## OFF TO MARKET

Every town of any size held a weekly market, where people from the surrounding villages came to sell their wares and buy any goods not available locally. Poultry, butter, eggs, cheese, grain, fish and livestock were all sold at markets which, like fairs, became great social gatherings.

## DOMESTIC COMFORTS

Life in the countryside was simple, but there was a growing level of sophistication as the country as a whole began to feel the benefits of increased foreign trade and travel. Domestic comforts increased as the quality of houses improved and higher wages meant that more people could eat healthier. Some could now afford meat and vegetables to add variety to their meagre diets. This picture shows a fish and sausage being grilled. The illustration on the right is a leather water bucket.

## VILLAGE LIFE

Village life had changed little since the Middle Ages. Most people did not venture far from home as villages were often self-contained. Villages had their own windmill to grind corn and local tradesmen making and selling goods not produced by the villagers themselves.

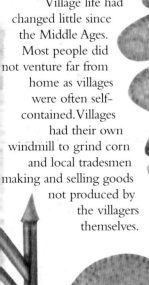

# LIFE IN TOWNS

*I*mproved methods of agriculture meant that fewer people were needed to work the land. Many peasants were evicted from their homes when their fields were sold off or turned over to sheep pasture for the rapidly expanding wool trade. The majority moved into towns to seek work as labourers for the growing number of merchants and traders who set up business there as a result of increased foreign trade. These changes occurred fairly quickly which meant overcrowding was a problem. Many of the houses were of inferior quality and crammed into narrow streets. Sanitation was poor and there were frequent outbreaks of disease, such as plague and cholera.

## FRESH WATER

Fresh drinking water in towns was difficult to obtain. Most people bought their supplies from water-carriers, who transported water in from the country.

# TUDOR
## & STUART LIFE

BY

JOHN GUY

# COUNTRY LIFE

Rustica

### HOME BREW

Most country households brewed their own wine, beer or cider. Any excess was transported to nearby towns in barrels on packhorses.

*W*hile poorer people still farmed strips of land in large, open fields and paid a tythe, or rent, to the church or local lord who owned the land, a new breed of farmer was emerging, called yeomen. They rented or bought several fields together to form small farms, usually on the outskirts of the village, and built themselves fine houses. They also employed labourers from the village to tend the fields instead of working on the land themselves and formed a 'middle class' of landowner, not so wealthy as the lords but much better off than the peasants.

'Plough

### WORKING THE LAND

Despite the growth of towns in both size and number, about 90% of the population still earned their living from the land.

### NATURAL CYCLES

Country life was dictated by natural cycles; by the seasons, the weather and the available daylight hours. Specific agricultural tasks had to be performed at certain times of the year. Here, peasants are pruning vines, usually undertaken each March.

Following the introduction of coffee into England from South America it quickly became a very fashionable, though expensive drink. Rich people met at 'coffee houses' in towns to exchange views and read newspapers (introduced in 1622 but only available in limited editions) or political pamphlets.

## FIRE

One of the biggest risks in towns was fire. Most of the buildings were made of wood and thatch, allowing the flames to spread easily. The Great Fire of London started on 2nd September 1666. It raged for five days unchecked, killing nine people and destroying over 13,000 buildings.

# LIFE FOR THE RICH

## FUNERAL HELM

Although changing methods of warfare had made armour an unnecessary encumbrance, many noblemen still owned a suit of elaborately decorated ceremonial armour, which they might wear at court or, as in this case, at their own funeral.

**B**y contrast, many people already comfortably off became very wealthy indeed, mostly as a result of increased foreign trade and exploitation as England began to extend its empire. With a strong government at home, many nobles replaced their austere castles with magnificent mansions, sparing no expense on the decorations and furnishings, or on their personal vanity, spending vast amounts of money on clothes and jewellery.

## COVER UP

To counteract the often unpleasant smells encountered around the house, or town, wealthy Tudor women carried a pomander, or scent bottle, on their belt. This silver-gilt example dates from c.1580 and had four separate compartments for different aromatic perfumes.

## A LOVETOKEN

Miniature portraits were specially commissioned by husbands and wives from wealthy families to be inserted in jewellery, such as this gold locket (c.1590), and carried as a love token.

### OLD BEFORE THEIR TIME

This painting of the Saltonstall family shows clearly the fashion for wealthy parents to dress children as young adults as soon as they were out of baby clothes.

## HOME COMFORTS

Furniture in Tudor and Stuart noble households became ever more elaborate and comfortable, typified by this exquisitely carved four-poster bed. Curtains could be lowered for privacy and warmth.

### ART FOR ART'S SAKE

With the opening up of the seaways in the 16th and 17th centuries vast fortunes were made, allowing the rich to adorn their houses with works of art. This elaborate, though impractical, 'Nautilus Cup' (c.1585) is made of silver gilt and shell.

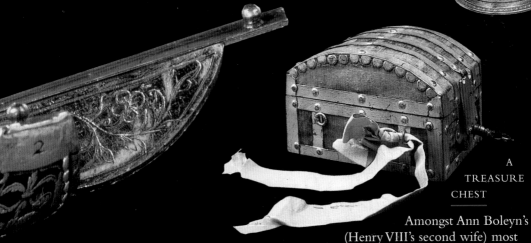

## A TREASURE CHEST

Amongst Ann Boleyn's (Henry VIII's second wife) most treasured possessions was her jewellery, which she carried with her on her frequent royal processions in this charming casket

# THE POOR AT HOME

*I*t is estimated that in the 16th and 17th centuries about half the population lived in poverty. Many resorted to begging, although it was illegal and they might be punished, or even hanged, if caught. Eventually, almshouses (similar to workhouses) were set up to help the poor, elderly and infirm who could no longer support themselves.

## TRADITIONAL ROLES

Traditionally, men and women in the poorer households all had to work and had their own specific responsibilities. The roles were clearly defined, the men working mostly in the fields and tending the livestock, while the women did the housework, cooked and made clothes. At busy times, such as harvesting, women would also be expected to help their husbands on the land.

## SUBSISTENCE LIVING

The poor often led a subsistence (or minimal) standard of living. Many still farmed the communal strips of land on the outskirts of the villages and kept a few chickens to supplement their income by selling the eggs. The husband and wife in this illustration are chasing away a fox about to kill one of their chickens.

## ARE YOU SITTING COMFORTABLY ?

Furniture was basic in poor households, usually consisting of a trestle table and bench seats. The suckling pig in the middle of the table indicates this is a special occasion.

## MEALTIMES

Only the well-off could afford pewter tableware, the poor had to content themselves with earthenware, often made by the householders themselves. This clay jug is typical and dates from about 1550-1600.

## IN THE NURSERY

One of the principal duties for women in the poorer households was looking after the children. Here, a mother is seen nursing a baby, with an older child alongside in a wooden pram.

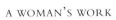

## A WOMAN'S WORK

Women also tended the poultry yard and carried out dairying tasks, including the production of milk, butter and cheese. Traditionally, they took their own excess produce to market and were allowed to keep the proceeds to spend as they wished.

# FOOD AND DRINK

The rich ate well with a wide variety of meats and vegetables regularly on the menu, including potatoes, recently introduced from America but still very expensive. Poorer classes had a more restricted diet of dairy produce, bread, basic vegetables and occasionally meat, such as rabbit. The rich drank wine at table, while the poor drank ale. Food was preserved in spices, or salt, though there were experiments with ice as a preservative by the late 17th century.

## A DELICACY

While we might frown upon it now, swans were considered a great delicacy for the rich. Poorer classes might content themselves with goose.

## FOOD DISPENSER

This fine piece of tableware is a Tudor peppermill recovered from the 'Mary Rose'.

## TABLE SERVICE

Retrieved from the wreck of the 'Mary Rose' this impressive collection of tableware shows the general level of sophistication practised at table by early Tudor times. The dishes and plates are of pewter, or wood.

## TABLE MANNERS

The children of Lord Cobham seated around the table are eating a variety of fresh fruits – with their pets wandering amongst the food !

## HARE TODAY, GAME TOMORROW

Hare and game birds, such as pheasant or partridge, were common additions to the rich man's table, while rabbits, caught wild, might supplement the poor man's diet.

## FOOD PREPARATION

The kitchen at Hampton Court shows how food was prepared (usually on wooden surfaces) in the 16th and 17th centuries. Cooking was still done mostly on open fires.

## 'GIN LANE'

Alcohol was cheap and excessive drinking amongst the poor, to ease the misery of poverty, became a problem, as this engraving by Hogarth shows.

## IMPROVING THE FLAVOUR

To improve the flavour of game, such as pheasant, deer and rabbit, it was hung in a cold room for several days before eating. Although still practised today, meat was then left until maggot-ridden to sweeten the taste.

# PASTIMES

Although people worked long hours, there were a lot of 'holy-days' (holidays) throughout the year when no-one was expected to work. People played a variety of games (for fun rather than as organised sports) such as hockey, cricket and football. The latter was played with a pig's bladder for a ball and was very different from today's game. Two teams from neighbouring villages met somewhere between the two communities. The object was to get the ball back to your own village - any way you could !

The theatre was popular, though women were not allowed to act, young boys taking women's roles.

## HITTING THE RIGHT NOTE

For people of all classes music has always played a prominent role as a source of entertainment, with professional musicians providing the music at court and dances. The Tudor period, however, saw the growth of individuals learning to play an instrument, or singing, for their own amusement.

## TREADING THE BOARDS

This picture shows the reconstructed open-air 'Globe Theatre'. The original was built in 1598-9 and was the most popular theatre in London. Shakespeare owned an eighth share in it and staged many of his plays there.

## THE BARD OF AVON

William Shakespeare (1564-1616), perhaps the best-known and greatest English dramatist, began his career, first as a stage hand in the Elizabethan theatre, then as an actor before going on to write plays.

## THE HUNT

Hawking and hunting remained popular pastimes throughout the Tudor and Stuart periods. Deer were the most popular quarry, but wild boar and wolves still roamed the countryside then and were considered fair game.

## BLOOD SPORTS

Bear-baiting, where dogs were set upon a tethered bear and bets made on the outcome, was a popular though cruel blood sport.

## BOARD GAMES

Board games were popular indoor pastimes. This backgammon board (known as tables) was found aboard the 'Mary Rose'.

## COMING UP TRUMPS

Card games were popular, both for pleasure and for gambling. The four players here are playing primero, an early forerunner of poker. The modern card pack is still based on Elizabethan court dress.

# FASHION

*F*ashion trends were greatly influenced by the monarch and court. The rich spent a lot of money on clothes. Elizabeth I had 260 gowns, 99 robes, 127 cloaks, 125 petticoats and hundreds of smaller accessories in her wardrobe. For the poor, coarse woollen clothes had to suffice, dyed one colour using vegetable dyes. But for the rich a range of materials was available, including linen and silk, which could be dyed or printed in a variety of colours and often richly embroidered. Women wore loose ruffs, while men exaggerated their stature by wearing huge, padded shoulders.

## LUCKY CHARM

Pendants, such as this one worn by Elizabeth I, were believed to be lucky charms to ward off evil and ill-health.

## LAYER UPON LAYER

Clothes for men were built up in layers for extra warmth. The nobleman in this picture wears leggings beneath a short tunic, with an inner and an outer cloak of ermine-lined red velvet.

## FINE JEWELS

Both men and women wore exquisite jewellery. Many fine jewels were imported with the opening up of new trade routes, such as this late-Medieval necklace from Russia.

## THE VIRGIN QUEEN (1558–1603)

Elizabeth I, daughter of Henry VIII by his second wife, Ann Boleyn, was ever conscious of being a woman in a male-dominated world. She was very particular about her appearance and is said to have taken a bath (then considered unwholesome) four times a year whether she needed it or not !

## BLACK TEETH

Many Tudor people had rotten teeth. However, one of the more unusual fashions of the time was the practice of deliberately blacking-out the front teeth, particularly among noble women. The practice may have developed to disguise genuinely rotten teeth.

## IF YOU CAN'T STAND THE HEAT

To disguise the pock scars of smallpox, candle wax was smoothed into the skin. The wax tended to melt if it came too close to the fire !

# ART AND ARCHITECTURE

**G**reat houses were usually built in brick, making them warmer and much more welcoming than their stone Medieval counterparts had been, with more attention paid to comfort and large windows to admit extra light. In the 17th century a Renaissance took place, with artists and architects reaching back to classical Rome for their inspiration. Gothic ideals were rejected in favour of the rounded arches and domes of buildings such as St. Paul's Cathedral in London, rebuilt by Sir Christopher Wren after the Medieval cathedral had been destroyed in the Great Fire of 1666.

SUMPTUOUS INTERIORS

With the advent of more settled times, more money could be spent on the interior comforts of castles and houses rather than on defensive features.

CHANGING STYLES

Ightham Mote, an unfortifi manor house in Kent, preserves a delightful blend of Medieval, Tudor and Jacobean domestic features.

RED-BRICK MANSION

Originally begun in 1515 by Cardinal Wolsey and given by him to Henry VIII, Hampton Court has been greatly extended by successive monarchs. It is a magnificent, luxuriously decorated palace with no defensive features whatsoever.

### LONG LIVE THE KING

This enigmatic oil painting of the Coronation Procession of Charles II in 1660
(by Dirck Stoop) shows an early and imaginative use of perspective.

### FURNITURE AS ART

This elaborately carved case
is made from imported
black ebony wood.
Each panel contains
a miniature painting
and bust.

### EVERY PICTURE
### TELLS A STORY

Portraiture first came to
prominence under the Tudors.
This study of Edward VI, by
an unknown artist, is typical of
the period. Tudor artists tried to
capture the expression of
feeling by visual impression.
By contrast with Medieval
paintings, which were
more symbolic, Tudor
works are more austere
and attempt to
flatter their
subjects.

# HEALTH AND MEDICINE

*T*here were frequent outbreaks of bubonic plague. The culprit was a species of flea, carried by rats aboard ships coming from the Middle East. Over 100,000 Londoners died in the 1665 outbreak alone. Diseases, especially epidemics such as the plague or cholera, were seen as divine punishment from God and magical remedies still featured strongly in any treatment to rid the patient of evil. Important breakthroughs in understanding human anatomy were made in the 17th century when the Church finally allowed dead bodies to be used for research.

## CRUEL TO BE KIND

Although it looks like he is being tortured, this patient is having a brain operation, without an anaesthetic.

## GREENWICH HOSPITAL

Greenwich Hospital stands on the site of the Tudor palace of Placentia, birthplace of Henry VI and Elizabeth I. It was rebuilt by Charles II, to designs by Sir Christopher Wren, and again by William III and Mary II. Mary founded the hospital in 1694 by Royal Charter, converting the unfinished palace buildings for th purpose. In 1873 the buildings were again converted for use as the Royal Naval College.

## BUBONIC PLAGUE

The popular children's rhyme: 'Ring-a-ring-o' roses,
A pocketful of posies, Atishoo, atishoo, We all
fall down', alludes to the plague. Garlands of
herbs were carried to ward off the
disease and sneezing was one of the
early symptoms. Death usually
followed within just five
days. The hand bell was
rung by undertakers
who collected
the dead.

## A MODERN EVIL

Although Sir John Hawkins
introduced tobacco into England
(from the American colonies in 1565)
it is Sir Walter Raleigh who made smoking
fashionable. It was smoked in clay pipes and
by the early 17th century there were 7000
shops selling tobacco in London alone.
Today about one in four smokers dies from
diseases directly caused by smoking.

## LIFE EXPECTANCY

This picture shows the five ages of man - baby, youth, adult, old age and finally
death. Child mortality was high, over half of those born dying in their first year.
Only one person in ten was expected to reach 40.

# LOVE AND MARRIAGE

*F*or most people marriage was more a matter of convenience than love. Many noblemen arranged the marriages of their children (particularly girls, who might be married as young as 12) in order to make political or monetary alliances. For the poorer classes it was often simply a matter of economics, girls looking for any man of prospects who might be able to support them.

When Charles II came back to the throne in 1660, following 11 years of repressive Puritan rule, a sexual revolution swept the land with the result that many inhibitions were dropped.

## COURTSHIP RITUALS

Young suitors of noble birth called upon their ladies at court (from where the modern word courtship derives) and conducted their romances under the supervision of chaperones.

## VOWS OF CHASTITY

Everyone entering into marriage took vows of chastity, but some husbands, particularly lords away at court, took them very seriously indeed. They made their wives wear a chastity belt to ensure they remained faithful, though they were free of course to do as they wished !

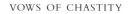

## MARRIAGE FEAST

This painting of a marriage feast at Bermondsey about 1569 gives a good impression of an Elizabethan society wedding. Festivities could go on for several days.

E OLDEST PROFESSION

men who fell on hard times,
example those widowed
ing and thus deprived of
income, might have to
ort to prostitution.
is woodcut (c.1600)
ws men gambling
an Elizabethan
thel.

A ROVING EYE

Charles II (the 'Merry
Monarch') was invited
by Parliament to
become king in 1660.
As part of the bargain
Charles had to marry
Catherine of Braganza,
from Portugal. It was a
loveless marriage and he
had many mistresses,
including the actress
Nell Gwynn,
pictured
here.

# WOMEN AND CHILDREN

Tudor and Stuart England was very much a male dominated society in which women and children had few rights. Wives were expected to obey their husbands and if they did not, or if they nagged, they might face the ducking stool as a punishment. Women were expected to help out in the fields, cook, keep house and mind the children. The only real profession open to them was nursing. Only children from wealthy families went to school, and then usually just the boys.

## CHILD'S PLAY

Although poorer children started work as young as six to help support the family, there was time to play. This toy gun is made of wood and is an authentic reproduction of a hand pistol.

## HORN BOOK

Children were taught to read using a simple horn book. A piece of paper, mounted on a wooden board, was covered by a thin sheet of transparent horn as protection.

## ALL IN A DAY'S WORK

This 17th century cottage interior shows a mother and grandmother carrying out cooking and laundry duties, while a child learns to walk in a wheeled baby walker.

## FUN AND GAMES

The boys in this picture (from a well-off family judging by the clothes) are playing a form of hop-scotch.

### 'BLOODY' MARY

Although Princess Mary was the first of Henry VIII's children to survive, women had few rights and succession to the throne was considered unseemly. She only succeeded to the throne following the death of Edward VI, her half-brother. She was a Catholic and had over 300 people executed for refusing to revert to Catholicism.

### A WOMAN'S LOT

Midwifery was one of the few professions open to women. Note the surgical instruments on the belt of the seated woman. The men in the background are calculating the astrological chart for the new baby.

### A TRAGIC AFFAIR

Lady Jane Grey was the cousin and childhood sweetheart of Edward VI. When he realised he was dying, he decided that she should rule after his death instead of his half-sister, Mary. She came to the throne at 16 and ruled for just nine days, before relinquishing the crown to Mary. She was later beheaded for treason.

### ORPHANS

Orphaned children had no rights whatsoever. For the lucky ones special courts appointed guardians, but many became vagabonds, relying on church charity for food.

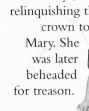

# WAR AND WEAPONRY

The Wars of the Roses were civil wars between the rival families of York and Lancaster, each claiming the English throne. Richard III lost his crown to Henry Tudor (House of Lancaster) who as Henry VII became the first Tudor monarch in 1485. When Henry VIII split with the Church of Rome he incurred the wrath of the Pope and lived under constant threat of invasion. Relations with Spain worsened in Elizabeth's reign when a massive armada was sent against England in 1588, which was routed by Sir Francis Drake. Charles I's attempt to rule without Parliament resulted in another Civil War (1642–46). He eventually lost the cause and was beheaded in 1649.

### 'MONS MEG'

This huge bombard, weighing over 8 tonnes, could fire a stone cannon ball a distance of nearly two miles.

### HUMILIATING DEFEAT

In the 17th century England was frequentl at war with Holland. Between 9-14th June 1667 the Dutch inflicted a humiliating defeat on the English navy by sailing up the River Medway, in Kent, and destroying many ships in the fleet

## KEEPING UP APPEARANCES

By the 16th and 17th centuries, with the development of guns, fighting armour was comparatively light, often consisting of breastplates and helmets only. Armour, such as this suit, harkened back to the middle ages and was more ceremonial than practical, used mostly for tournaments.

## YEOMEN OF THE GUARD

Following Henry VII's victory at Bosworth Field in 1485 several attempts were made on his life. As a precaution, he established a personal bodyguard unit of yeomen at the Tower of London. Their successors still wear the same scarlet uniforms today.

## THE ROUTE OF THE ARMADA

Following their famous defeat in August 1588 the Spanish Armada took flight northwards, around the coast of Scotland. Of 130 ships, only 70 returned home to Spain.

## CIVIL WAR

Oliver Cromwell was a farmer before joining the Puritan army. He led the Parliamentarians against the Royalists in the Civil War (1642–49) of Charles I's reign. The king was beheaded in 1649 and England became a republic under Cromwell.

# CRIME AND PUNISHMENT

The increased trade and improved agricultural methods, as well as bringing prosperity to some, also created a crime wave from those whose livelihoods were threatened. The population rose, but fewer people were required to work the land. Many landlords turned peasants out of their homes, converting their fields and common lands into sheep pasture. It is estimated that by 1560 there were more than 10,000 homeless people wandering the countryside looking for work. Many resorted to begging, while others turned to crime, even though harsh punishments were introduced to curb the trend.

### FLOGGING

Flogging was a common punishment for a number of minor offences, such as stealing, or even simply being caught begging.

### HENRY VIII'S IRON RULE

When Henry VIII divorced his first wife, Catherine of Aragon, and broke from the Church of Rome, there was the constant threat of rebellion. He ruled the land with an iron fist and is estimated to have executed several thousand people (though no accurate records exist) mostly because of their religious or political beliefs.

## ROYAL PRIVILEGE

Royal prisoners who had been condemned to death, reserved the right to be beheaded by an executioner using a sword, instead of an axe, as it was considered more dignified. Ann Boleyn chose this method at her execution in 1536.

## A SENSE OF JUSTICE

Taxation was high and punishments severe. Most towns had a court where Justices of the Peace, who travelled the land, heard criminal cases, but they were unpaid and therefore open to corruption.

## OFF WITH THEIR HEADS

The block and axe was usually reserved for nobility and political prisoners for crimes against the Crown. Victims knelt before the block, with arms outstretched, but the axe was seldom sharp enough to sever the head with one blow.

## DEATH BY STONING

Adulterers, or those committing 'crimes' against the Church, were sometimes executed by stoning, or by crushing, having heavy stones piled onto their chests.

# TRANSPORT
# AND SCIENCE

ravel was very difficult, and dangerous, throughout the 16th and 17th centuries. Some of the main roads had metalled surfaces, but most were little more than beaten earth, which became very muddy and impassable in winter months. Most people walked or went on horseback because carriages were still very uncomfortable. In towns, the rich were conveyed in Sedan chairs, similar to a small carriage but with handrails instead of wheels, carried by two men. Toll roads were introduced in 1663 to raise money to improve the roads. The 17th century saw many important new discoveries in the field of science, including research into human anatomy by William Harvey and into physics and gravity by Sir Isaac Newton.

### HEARTS OF OAK

English shipwrights became world leaders in designing ships to carry cannon, helping seafarers like Drake, Raleigh and Frobisher to gain supremacy of the open seas. Many were built at the royal dockyards of Chatham and Woolwich, where there was an abundant supply of trees. The oak forests of Kent and Sussex were not cleared to provide the timber, but carefully managed as a crop.

### HIDDEN WORLDS

With the invention of the microscope, scientists could see tiny creatures and organisms, such as this flea, scarcely visible to the human eye, for the first time in dazzling detail.

## ΉE SORCERER'S APPRENTICE

Ichemists believed they could
ansform base metals into gold and,
though unsuccessful, they advanced
e study of chemistry considerably,
articularly in medicine.

## MICROSCOPIC DETAIL

This late 17th century compʊ
microscope is similar to one
the eminent physicist Robeⁱ
Hooke. For the first
time microscopic
creatures, too
small to be
seen with the
human eye,
could be
observed.

## IT'S IN
THE STARS

Instruments
such as this
brass astronomical
compendium, made
in 1569, were used for accurate
navigation. They were also used to make
astrological charts, which were taken
very seriously.

## DAWNING OF A NEW AGE

It is not generally acknowledged
that the Stuart period marked the
beginning of the modern industrial
age. This atmospheric
engine, used to pump
water from mines,
was developed by
Newcomen and
dates from 1705.

# RELIGION

The 16th and 17th centuries were periods of great upheaval and reform in the Church. There was already a growing number of people who objected (Protestants) to the Catholic faith before Henry VIII's break with Rome. When Henry failed to get a divorce from Catherine of Aragon by the Pope he established a separate Church of England with himself as head though he remained a staunch Catholic throughout his life. The Protestants rallied to the new Church, which eventually became accepted as a Protestant faith.

### CHURCH REFORMS

Pilgrimages to religious shrines were outlawed by the 17th century church reformers who stripped them from the churches.

### PURITAN REFORMS

Following the Reformation of the Church by the Tudo[r] most church decoration, such as this colourful triptyc[h] (altar piece) was removed by the Puritans.

### A FAIR TRIAL?

Anyone accused of witchcraft was ducked under water. If they drowned, they were considered innocent, but if they survived they were deemed to be a witch and subsequently executed !

### DISSOLUTION OF THE MONASTERIES

Following alleged corruption within the monasteries (but more likely as an excuse to seize their wealth) Henry VIII closed them down between 1536-40.

## E GUNPOWDER PLOT

group of Catholic conspirators,
ed by Guido (Guy) Fawkes, an
plosives expert, tried unsuccessfully
blow up Parliament and the
otestant James I.

## HE FIRST
## JGLISH BIBLE

he Catholic missal
as replaced by the
st English Book of
ommon Prayer in
649, following Henry
III's break with the
hurch of Rome.

## CARDINAL WOLSEY
## (1475–1530)

Cardinal Wolsey
enjoyed a meteoric
rise to fame and
fortune as Henry
VIII's Lord
Chancellor. He fell
out of royal favour,
however, when he
failed to secure
Henry's divorce from
Catherine of Aragon.
He was arrested
and ordered to
the Tower of
London for
trial, but he
died en
route.

# A GLOSSARY OF
# INTERESTING TERMS

**Gay** - In the middle ages and up to Tudor times, the word girl meant any young person, male or female. To differentiate between the genders males were known as knave-girls, and females as gay-girls. A boy who thus acted in an effeminate manner was called a 'gay-girl' instead of a knave-girl.

**Idiot** - The word idiot was originally used to describe an ordinary person, or a layman, as opposed to a clergyman. Since most laymen were uneducated the word gradually came to describe ignorant or foolish people.

**Backlog** - Today, the word backlog means an unwanted build-up, but in Tudor times, and before, it was considered a good thing. It was a reserve to fall back on when needed: the back-log placed on a fire to keep it burning.

**Off the beaten track** - Most roads were not constructed as such, but comprised of beaten earth. When they became impassable in the winter, travellers left the road in search of a better route - off the beaten track.

**Hooker** - The original meaning of this word was a thief who used a long pole with a hook on the end to steal washing from clothes lines.

**Spinster** - If a girl did not marry or enter the church as a nun, she had to remain living with her parents and help with the chores, especially spinning, a dull and repetitive job. Unmarried women soon earned the name spinners, or spinsters.

**Jus primae noctis** - Was the right of a lord to be the first to sleep with a bride on her wedding night - even before the groom. It was widely practised throughout Europe but was gradually outlawed with the abolition of serfdom at the end of the Middle Ages. As landlords, this 'privilege' was even accorded to the clergy !

**Alchemy** - The science of trying to transform base metals into gold. Although unsuccessful, alchemists advanced the study of chemistry considerably, particularly in medicine, and were the forerunners of modern pharmacists.

## ACKNOWLEDGEMENTS

We would like to thank: Graham Rich and Elizabeth Wiggans for their assistance and David Hobbs for his map of the world.
**Copyright © 2004 *ticktock* Media Ltd,**
Unit 2, Orchard Business Centre North Farm Road, Tunbridge Wells, Kent TN2 3XF, U.K. First published in Great Britain 1998.
All rights reserved. No part of this publication may be reproduced, stored in a retrieval system, or transmitted in any form or by any means electronic, mechanical, photocopying, recording or otherwise, without prior written permission of the copyright owner.
Picture research by Image Select. Printed in China.

Acknowledgements: Picture Credits  t=top, b=bottom, c=centre, l=left, r=right
Abbreviation: BAL=Bridgeman Art Library
Ann Ronan at Image Select; 2cl, 10bl, 22bc, 23bl, 29bl. Asprey & Co., London/BAL; OBCbr/8c. Barnaby's Picture Library; OFCr/25l. Bodleian Library; 2tl/3c (Roll 156B. frame 9), 2bl (163C.7), 3b (156B.25), 4tl (263.3.3), 6b (263.3.4), 6/7t (156B.17), OBCtl/7br (263.3.8), 7cr (165E.14), 7tr (163C.2), 9tl (156B.68), 10cl (156B.58), 12/13c (156B.64), 18/19ct (156B.78), 19b (209.10), 20tl (163C.12), OBCr/23tl (163C.16), OBCbl/26tl (215.3.12), 26/27c (163C.15), 27tr (215.3.16), 29tl (209.9), 30tl (163C.17). British Library, London/BAL; OFCc. British Museum, London/BAL; OFCtl/14tl. Collection of the Earl of Derby, Suffolk/BAL; 13br. E.T. Archive; 5tr, 9/10ct. Filkins, London/BAL; OBCtl/7c. Fitzwilliam Museum, University of Cambridge/BAL; 9cr. Fotomas Index; 23c. Guildhall Art Gallery, Corporation of London/BAL; 23br. Hatfield House, Hertfordshire/BAL; 20bl. Hermitage, St. Petersburg/BAL; 12l. © Historic Royal Palaces (Crown Copyright); 10r, 10c, 16bl. © Historic Scotland; 24tl. Hulton Deutsch Collection Ltd.; 20/21c. Kremlin Museums, Moscow/BAL; 14/15b. © Leeds Castle Foundation; OFCbr/9br, 26bl, 30cr, 31bl. Manor House, Stanton Harcourt, Oxon/BAL; 27tl. Mary Evans Picture Library; 13cr, 20/21ct. © Mary Rose Trust; 9cr, 9bl, 13bl. Mittelalterliches Kriminalmuseum; 30bl. Museum of London; 18/19c, 22/23c. Museum of London/BAL; 4/5, 17t. National Maritime Museum, London; 15tr, 18bl, 24/25c, 24bl, 28cl, 28/29c. National Trust Photographic Library/Ian Shaw; 16c. Philip Mould, Historical Portraits Ltd., London/BAL; 21. Prado, Madrid/BAL; 23tr. Private Collection/BAL; 9tl. Reproduced by kind permission of the President and Council of the Royal College of Surgeons of London; 18tl. Reproduced by permission of Viscount de L'Isle from his private collection; IFC/1. Richard Kalina; 12/13ct. Royal Armouries; 27b. Tate Gallery, London; 9tr. The Mansell Collection; 2/3t, 22br. The National Portrait Gallery, London; OFCr/13tr, OBCr/19cr, 25bl, 31r. The Science Museum/Science & Society Picture Library; OFCbl/28b, OFCtr/29r. Victoria & Albert Museum, London/BAL; 9cl.

Every effort has been made to trace the copyright holders and we apologise in advance for any unintentional omissions. We would be pleased to insert the appropriate acknowledgement in any subsequent edition of this publication.

A CIP Catalogue for this book is available from the British Library. ISBN 1 86007 403 0